John R. Sweney

Royal Fountain - no. 4

sacred songs and hymns for use in Sabbath-school or prayer meeting

John R. Sweney

Royal Fountain - no. 4
sacred songs and hymns for use in Sabbath-school or prayer meeting

ISBN/EAN: 9783337265427

Printed in Europe, USA, Canada, Australia, Japan

Cover: Foto ©Lupo / pixelio.de

More available books at **www.hansebooks.com**

THE ROYAL FOUNTAIN,

No. 4.

SACRED SONGS AND HYMNS

FOR USE IN

Sabbath-School or Prayer Meeting,

BY

JNO. R. SWENEY AND WM. J. KIRKPATRICK.

Philadelphia: JOHN J. HOOD, 1018 Arch St.

COPYRIGHT, 1884, BY JOHN J. HOOD.

THE ROYAL FOUNTAIN.

The New Jerusalem.

"Our feet shall stand within thy gates, O Jerusalem."

Rev. Wm. H. Hunter, D. D.   Jno. R. Sweney.

1. Jerusalem! thy mansions fair Ignoble souls may never share;
For all who walk thy streets of gold Are in the book of life enroll'd.

2. Whoso from earth would thither go, Must wash his robes as white as snow;—
In Jesus' blood, the fount of grace, Find pure, unspotted righteousness.

CHORUS.
O, Jerusalem! O, Jerusalem! Our feet within thy gates shall stand! O, Jerusalem! New Jerusalem!

3. O Lamb of God, my heart prepare,
To enter with the holy there;
Within thy book my name enroll,
And write thine own upon my soul.

3. To him that loves and trusts the Lord,
And keeps with patient hope his word,
The Spirit with his spirit bears
Sweet witness to his answered prayers.

5. Whoever has this seal of love
His title reads to seats above;
And looking upward as he runs,
The taint of sinful pleasure shuns.

6. Jesus, fulfil my long desire
To stand with thee in pure attire,
And find at last a place and name
Within the New Jerusalem.

Copyright, 1877, by JOHN J. HOOD.

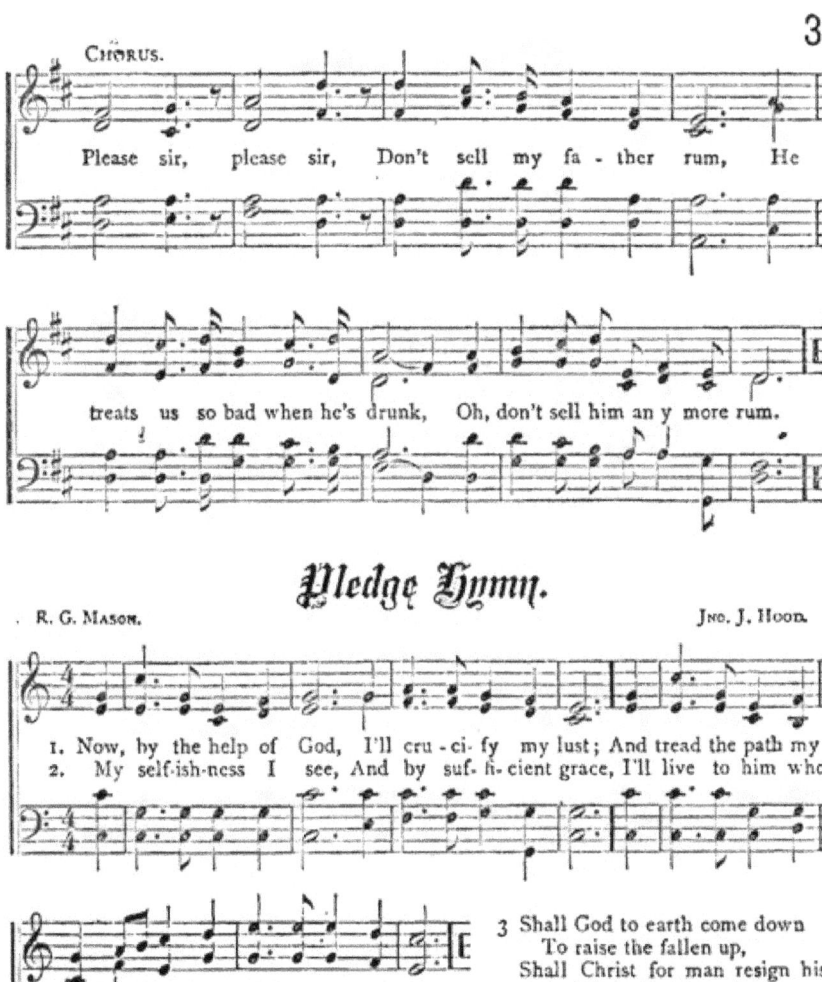

Pledge Hymn.

R. G. Mason.   Jno. J. Hood.

1. Now, by the help of God, I'll crucify my lust; And tread the path my Saviour trod, And in Jehovah trust.
2. My selfishness I see, And by sufficient grace, I'll live to him who died for me, And benefit my race.
3. Shall God to earth come down To raise the fallen up, Shall Christ for man resign his crown, And I retain my cup?
4. 'Tis done! I've snapp'd the spell, And left the slave behind: To demonizing drink farewell,— The covenant is signed.

I HEAR THY WELCOME VOICE.—Key E♭.

1. I hear thy welcome voice
That calls me, Lord, to thee,
For cleansing in thy precious blood
That flowed on Calvary.
CHORUS.
I am coming, Lord,
Coming now to thee!
Wash me, cleanse me in the blood
That flowed on Calvary.

2. Though coming weak and vile,
Thou dost my strength assure;
Thou dost my vileness fully cleanse,
Till spotless all and pure.

3. 'Tis Jesus calls me on
To perfect faith and love,
To perfect hope, and peace, and trust,
For earth and heaven above.

4. Come and Sign.

J. H. Jackson.
Jno. R. Sweney.

1. Come and sign the pledge,— 'Tis no-ble to ab-stain;
2. Fall-en and de-spised, Is this your true e-state?
3. Heaven will grace af-ford To conquer ev'-ry sin;

For-ev-er crush the de-mon lust, That wrecks the heart and brain.
God willeth not that an-y soul Should meet a drunkard's fate.
Now ac-cept, and from this hour, A pur-er life be-gin.

CHORUS.

Come and sign, Come and sign, Take this no-ble vow,
vow, take this vow,
Trust in God, He'll grace af-ford, He waits to bless you now.

Follow the Lamb.

REV. WM. HUNTER, D. D. The last melody by the late lamented REV. J. H. STOCKTON.

1. O Jesus, immaculate Lamb! Thy faultless example I see,
2. Thy word would I firmly believe, Thy footsteps unswerving pursue,

And, conscious how feeble I am, For help look alone unto thee.
Thy spirit of meekness receive, Thy will with all diligence do.

CHORUS.

Oh, follow the Lamb! Follow the holy Lamb! To the
  spotless Lamb,   spotless Lamb,

living fountains he leads, Follow, oh, follow the Lamb!

3 Thy love in my heart shed abroad,
   A flame of pure loyalty there;
   A zeal for the glory of God,
   Kept burning by watching and prayer.
      Oh, follow the Lamb!

4 Thyself in my bosom enshrine,
   The Lord of my passions and will;
   And all my new nature incline
   Thy law with delight to fulfil.
      Oh, follow the Lamb!

5 No virtue of mine can I claim,
   No power to perform what I would;
   The virtue is all in thy name,   [blood.
   The power comes alone through thy
      Oh, follow the Lamb!

6 Oh, save me completely from sin,
   Oh, wash me, and I shall be pure;
   A thorough renewal within,
   A perfect and permanent cure.
      Oh, follow the Lamb!

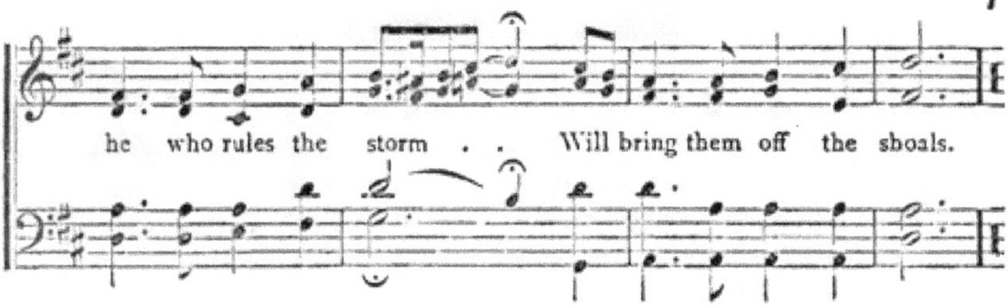

he who rules the storm .. Will bring them off the shoals.

In the Silent Midnight Watches.

Rev. A. C. Coxe, D. D.   Jno. R. Sweney.

1. In the silent midnight watches, List thy bosom's door, How there knocketh,
2. Death comes down with reckless footsteps to the hall and hut; Think you death will

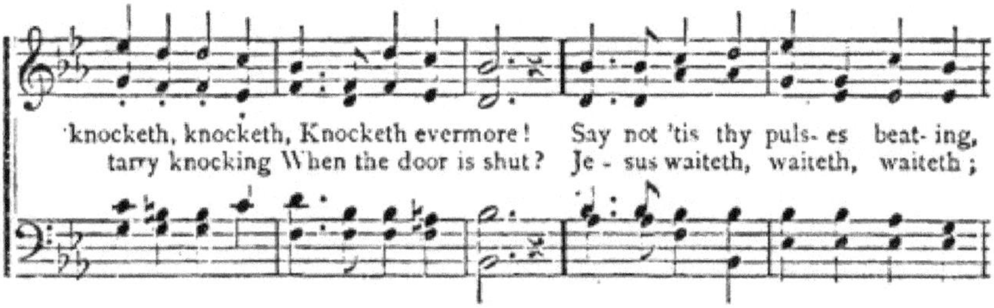

knocketh, knocketh, Knocketh evermore! Say not 'tis thy puls-es beat-ing,
tarry knocking When the door is shut? Je-sus waiteth, waiteth, waiteth;

'Tis thy heart of sin;—'Tis thy Saviour knocks, and crieth, 'Rise and let me in!'
But the door is fast; Grieved, away thy Saviour goeth, Death breaks in at last.

3 Then 'tis time to stand entreating
   Christ to let *thee* in;
At the gate of heaven beating,
   Wailing for thy sin!
Nay: alas! thou guilty creature,
   Hast thou, then forgot?
Jesus waited long to know thee,
   Now he knows thee not.

4 Think, then, while thy pulse is beating,
   And thy heart of sin,
How thy Saviour stands and crieth,
   'Rise and let me in,'
How he knocketh, knocketh, knocketh,
   Knocketh evermore,
In the silent midnight watches,
   At thy bosom's door.

2 His faithful ones, who ever strive
    His righteous cause to win,
   Shall see their Master's work revive,
    His vict'ry over sin.
   A fallen world in darkness lies,
    Each to the rescue speeds;
   Though foes on every side arise,
    Remember Jesus leads.

3 Go up against sin's fortress walls,
    Go in the strength of grace;
   And if a standard-bearer falls,
    Then you must take his place.
   Oh, tell his love, that cannot fail,
    Make known his glorious deeds,
   And tho' you walk thro' death's dark
    Remember Jesus leads.   [vale,

From "Leaflet Gems, No. 1," by per.

I Will Rise.

JNO. R. SWENEY.

rise, I will rise, I will rise and go, For my Father's
wasted the gifts that he gave me, and yet, The love of my
me of my Fa-ther is wondrous-ly fair, Its towers seem to

welcome, I know, There is light and love,—all is sha-dow
sure-ly for-get; I have fed on husks, he hath bread and to
vi-sions of care, I fan-cy he stands at the wide open

CHORUS.

sob my sins in a Fa-ther's ear, Saying, my Fa-ther,
go in my shame, and my want, and despair, Saying, etc.
atch for the child who will seek it heart-sore, Saying, etc.

Fa-ther, saying, my Father, I have sinned 'gainst thee; O

Father, have mer-cy, on me, E-ven on me, e-ven on me.

4.   5.
s, and deep as the sea, | Unworthy, unworthy the least of his grace,
her to sinners like me ; | I'll plead as a servant to look on his face :
at a beggar would shun, | His love will enfold me, his heart is my home;
called his son, etc. | Tho' I die at thy feet, O my Father, I come.

Rock of Ages.

TOPLADY.   JNO. R. SWENEY.

1. Rock of Ages, cleft for me, Let me hide myself in thee; Let the water and the blood From thy wounded side which flowed, Be of sin the double cure, Save from wrath, and make me pure.

CHORUS.

Rock of A-ges, Rock of A-ges, Let me hide my-self in thee,
Rock of A-ges, Rock of A-ges, Let me hide my-self in thee.

2 Could my tears forever flow,—
Could my zeal no languor know,
All for sin could not atone,
Thou must save, and thou alone:
In my hand no price I bring;
Simply to thy cross I cling.

3 While I draw this fleeting breath,
When my eyes shall close in death,
When I soar to worlds unknown,
See thee on thy judgment throne,—
Rock of Ages, cleft for me,
Let me hide myself in thee,

Believing.

C. WESLEY. Rev. J. H. STOCKTON.

1. Jesus, thine all victorious love Shed in my heart abroad;
Then shall my feet no longer rove, Rooted and fixed in God.

CHORUS.

I'm believing, I'm believing, Believing now in the Lord;
I'm believing, and receiving Salvation through his blood.

2 O that in me the sacred fire
Might now begin to glow;
Burn up the dross of base desire,
And make the mountains flow.

3 O that it now from heaven might fall,
And all my sins consume:
Come, Holy Ghost, for thee I call;
Spirit of burning, come.

4 Refining fire, go through my heart:
Illuminate my soul;
Scatter thy life in every part,
And sanctify the whole.

5 My steadfast soul, from falling free,
Shall then no longer move;
While Christ is all the world to me,
And all my heart is love.

ALAS! AND DID MY SAVIOUR BLEED? C. M.

1 Alas! and did my Saviour bleed?
And did my Sov'reign die?
Would he devote that sacred head
For such a worm as I?

CHORUS.

Help me, dear Saviour, thee to own,
And ever faithful be;
And when thou sittest on thy throne,
O Lord, remember me.

2 Was it for crimes that I have done
He groaned upon the tree!
Amazing pity! grace unknown!
And love beyond degree!

3 Well might the sun in darkness hide,
And shut his glories in,
When Christ, the mighty Maker, died
For man, the creature,'s sin.

4 Thus might I hide my blushing face
While his dear cross appears;
Dissolve my heart in thankfulness,
And melt mine eyes to tears.

5 But drops of grief can ne'er repay
The debt of love I owe;
Here, Lord, I give myself away,—
'Tis all that I can do.

* From "Precious Songs," by per.

The Rifted Rock.

Mary D. James. Jno. R. Sweney.

1. In the Rift-ed Rock I'm resting, Safe-ly shelter'd I a-bide,
2. Long pur-sued by sin and Sa-tan, Wea-ry, sad, I long'd for rest,

There no foes nor storms mo-lest me, While within the cleft I hide.
Then I found this heavenly shelter, O-pen'd in my Sa-viour's breast.

CHORUS.

Now I'm resting, sweet-ly rest-ing, In the cleft once made for me;
Je-sus, bles-sed Rock of A-ges, I will hide my-self in thee.

3 Peace which passeth understanding,
   Joy the world can never give
Now in Jesus I am finding,
   In his smiles of love I live.
     Now I'm resting, etc.

4 In the Rifted Rock I'll hide me
   Till the storms of life are past,
All secure in this blest refuge,
   Heeding not the fiercest blast.
     Now I'm resting, etc.

The Great Physician.

Rev. Wm. H. Hunter, D.D. Arranged by J. H. Stockton.

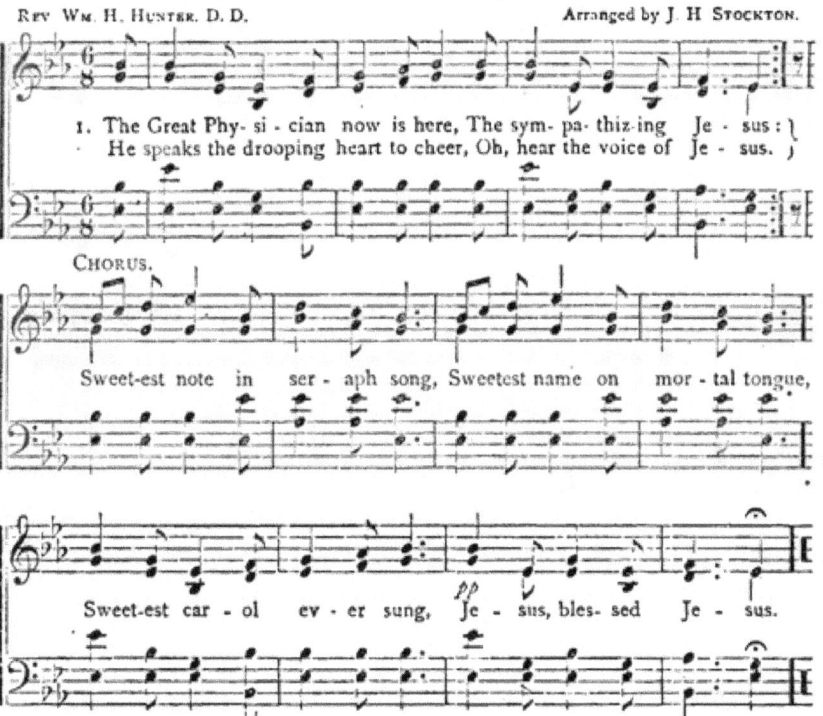

1. The Great Phy-si-cian now is here, The sym-pa-thiz-ing Je-sus:
He speaks the drooping heart to cheer, Oh, hear the voice of Jesus.

CHORUS.
Sweet-est note in ser-aph song, Sweetest name on mor-tal tongue,
Sweet-est car-ol ev-er sung, Je-sus, bles-sed Je-sus.

2 Your many sins are all forgiven,
Oh, hear the voice of Jesus;
Go on your way in peace to heaven,
And wear a crown with Jesus.

3 All glory to the dying Lamb!
I now believe in Jesus;
I love the blessed Saviour's name,
I love the name of Jesus.

4 The children too, both great and small,
Who love the name of Jesus,
May now accept his gracious call
To work and live for Jesus.

5 Come, brethren, help me sing his praise,
Oh, praise the name of Jesus;
Come, sisters, all your voices raise,
Oh, bless the name of Jesus.

6 His name dispels my guilt and fear,
No other name but Jesus;
Oh, how my soul delights to hear
The precious name of Jesus.

7 And when to that bright world above,
We rise to see our Jesus,
We'll sing around the throne of love
His name, the name of Jesus.

MY SOUL, BE ON THY GUARD.—Laban, key D.

1 My soul, be on thy guard,
Ten thousand foes arise;
The hosts of sin are pressing hard
To draw thee from the skies.

2 Oh, watch, and fight, and pray;
The battle ne'er give o'er;
Renew it boldly every day,
And help divine implore.

3 Ne'er think the vict'ry won,
Nor lay thine armor down;
The work of faith will not be done
Till thou obtain the crown.

4 Then persevere till death
Shall bring thee to thy God;
He'll take thee, at thy parting breath,
To his divine abode.

Yield not to Temptation.
H. R. PALMER. By per.

1. Yield not to tempta-tion, For yielding is sin, Each victr'y will help you some oth-er to win; Fight manfully onward, Dark passions sub-due,
2. Shun e-vil companions, Bad language disdain, God's name hold in rev'rence, nor take it in vain; Be thoughtful and earnest, Kind-hearted and true,
3. To him that o'ercometh God giveth a crown, Thro' faith we will conquer, though often cast down; He who is our Saviour, Our strength will renew,

CHORUS.

Look ev-er to Je-sus, He'll car-ry you through. Ask the Saviour to help you, Comfort, strengthen, and keep you, He is willing to aid you, He will carry you through.

STAND UP FOR JESUS.—*Webb, key B flat.*

1 Stand up! stand up for Jesus!
  Ye soldiers of the cross;
  Lift high his royal banner,
  It must not suffer loss;
  From victory unto victory
  His army he shall lead,
  Till every foe is vanquished,
  And Christ is Lord indeed.

2 Stand up! stand up for Jesus!
  Stand in his strength alone;
  The arm of flesh will fail you,—
  Ye dare not trust your own;
  Put on the gospel armor,
  And, watching unto prayer,
  Where duty calls, or danger,
  Be never wanting there.

3 Stand up! stand up for Jesus!
  The strife will not be long;
  This day the noise of battle,
  The next the victor's song;
  To him that overcometh
  A crown of life shall be,
  He with the King of Glory
  Shall reign eternally.

ONLY TRUST HIM.—Key G.

1 Come, every soul by sin oppressed,
   There's mercy with the Lord,
And he will surely give you rest,
   By trusting in his word.
   CHORUS.
Only trust him, only trust him,
   Only trust him now;
He will save you, he will save you,
   He will save you now.

2 For Jesus shed his precious blood
   Rich blessings to bestow;
Plunge now into the crimson tide
   That washes white as snow.

3 Yes, Jesus is the Truth, the Way,
   That leads you into rest;
Believe in him without delay,
   And you are fully blest.

I've been Redeemed.

Plantation Melody.   Arr. by Dr. T. H. Peacock.   By per.

1. There is a fountain filled with blood Drawn from Immanuel's veins, And sinners plunged beneath that flood - - - Lose all their guilty stains.
2. The dying thief rejoiced to see That fountain in his day, And there have I, tho' vile as he, - - - Washed all my sins away.

CHORUS.
I've been redeem'd, I've been redeem'd, I've been redeem'd, I've been redeem'd,
Been wash'd in the blood of the Lamb. Been redeem'd by the blood of the Lamb,
Been redeem'd by the blood of the Lamb, That flow'd on Cal-va-ry.

ALL TO CHRIST I OWE.—Key E♭.

1. I hear the Saviour say,
Thy strength indeed is small;
Child of weakness, watch and pray,
Find in me thine all in all.

Cho.—*Jesus paid it all,*
   All to him I owe;
   Sin had left a crimson stain,
   He washed it white as snow.

2. Lord, now indeed I find
Thy power, and thine alone,
Can change the leper's spots,
And melt the heart of stone.

3. For nothing good have I
Whereby thy grace to claim,—
I'll wash my garment white
In the blood of Calvary's Lamb.

4. When from my dying bed
My ransomed soul shall rise,
Then "Jesus paid it all"
Shall rend the vaulted skies.

5. And when before the throne
I stand in him complete,
I'll lay my trophies down,
All down at Jesus' feet.

It Reaches Me.

MARY D. JAMES.   JNO. R. SWENEY.

1. Oh, this ut-ter-most sal-va-tion! 'Tis a foun-tain full and free,
2. How a-maz-ing God's compas-sion, That so vile a worm should prove
3. Je-sus, Sav-iour, I a-dore thee! Now thy love I will pro-claim,

Pure, ex-haustless, ev-er flow-ing, Wondrous grace! it reaches me!
This stupend-ous bliss of Heav-en, This un-meas-ured wealth of love!
I will tell the blessed sto-ry, I will mag-ni-fy thy name!

CHORUS.

It reaches me! it reaches me! Wondrous grace! it reaches me!

Pure, ex-haustless, ev-er flow-ing, Wondrous grace! it reaches me!

AM I A SOLDIER OF THE CROSS. C. M.

1 Am I a soldier of the cross,—
A foll'wer of the Lamb,—
And shall I fear to own his cause,
Or blush to speak his name?

2 Must I be carried to the skies
On flowery beds of ease;
While others fought to win the prize,
And sailed through bloody seas?

3 Are there no foes for me to face?
Must I not stem the flood?
Is this vile world a friend to grace,
To help me on to God?

4 Since I must fight if I would reign,
Increase my courage, Lord;
I'll bear the toil, endure the pain,
Supported by thy Word.

Come to the Royal Fountain.

Wm. H. Clark. Wm J. Kirkpatrick.

1. See where the liv-ing waters glide, From David's house they sweetly flow;
Who wash-es in the cleansing tide Is whit-er than the driven snow.

CHORUS.
Then, come to the roy-al foun-tain! Ev-er in its stream a-bide;
Come to the roy-al foun-tain, O-pen'd in the Sav-iour's side.

2 It flows, an ever-running stream,—
Free as the fountain of his grace
Who died, that he might thus redeem
The fallen sons of Adam's race.

3 Down through the ages flowing wide,—
Its virtue is to-day the same
As when from out his pierced side
The mingled tide of blessing came.

4 Whoever will, may drink and live;
New life the healing draught inspires;
From those who nothing have to give,
The royal bounty naught requires.

5 All over Canaan's goodly land,
Where saints enjoy a sweet repose,
'Mid pastures green, on every hand
King David's royal fountain flows.

From "Leaflet Gems, No. 1," by per.

Bless Me, O Thou Bleeding Lamb.

Behold the Lamb of God, which taketh away the sins of the world.

Rev. W. H. Luckenbach. Jno. R. Sweney.

1. To thee, O Lamb of God, to thee I come, with all my fears;
   With all the sins that burden me, In penitence and tears.
2. Thy open wounds supply the balm That heals the suff'ring heart;
   'Tis only this, thou precious Lamb, Can life and health impart.

CHORUS.
Oh, receive me, Lord, I pray, Weak and sinful though I am;
Take, oh, take my sins away; Bless me, O thou bleeding Lamb!

3 Be merciful, O Lamb of God,
  Hear this, my only plea,—
  That thou canst cleanse me by thy blood,—
  Have mercy then on me.

4 Thy saving blood, of greater worth
  Than aught the world hath given,
  Shall be my last blest song on earth,
  And first glad theme in heaven.

From "Goodly Pearls," by per.

HE LEADETH ME.—Key D.

1 He leadeth me! oh, blessed thought!
Oh, words with heavenly comfort fraught!
Whate'er I do, where'er I be,
Still 'tis God's hand that leadeth me.
REFRAIN.
He leadeth me! he leadeth me!
By his own hand he leadeth me;
His faithful follower I would be,
For by his hand he leadeth me.

2 Sometimes mid scenes of deepest gloom,
Sometimes where Eden's bowers bloom,
By waters still, o'er troubled sea,—
Still 'tis his hand that leadeth me.

3 Lord, I would clasp thy hand in mine,
Nor ever murmur nor repine,—
Content, whatever lot I see,
Since 'tis my God that leadeth me.

4 And when my task on earth is done,
When by thy grace the victory's won,
E'en death's cold wave I will not flee,
Since God through Jordan leadeth me.

Deliverance will Come.

Words arr.
Melody by Rev. W. M'Donald. By per.

I saw a way-worn trav'ler, In tat-ter'd garments clad,
His back was la-den heavy, His strength was al-most gone,
And struggling up the mountain, It seemed that he was sad;
Yet he shout-ed as he jour-ney'd, De-liv-er-ance will come.

CHORUS.

Then palms of vic-to-ry, crowns of glory, Palms of victo-ry I shall wear.

2 The summer sun was shining,
　The sweat was on his brow,
　His garments worn and dusty,
　His step seemed very slow:
　But he kept pressing onward,
　For he was wending home;
　Still shouting as he journeyed,
　Deliverance will come!

3 The songsters in the arbor
　That stood beside the way
　Attracted his attention,
　Inviting his delay:
　His watchword being "Onward!"
　He stopped his ears and ran,
　Still shouting as he journeyed,
　Deliverance will come!

4 I saw him in the evening,
　The sun was bending low,
　He'd overtopped the mountain
　And reached the vale below:
　He saw the golden city,—
　His everlasting home,—
　And shouted loud, Hosanna,
　Deliverance will come!

5 While gazing on that city,
　Just o'er the narrow flood,
　A band of holy angels
　Came from the throne of God:
　They bore him on their pinions
　Safe o'er the dashing foam,
　And joined him in his triumph,—
　Deliverance has come!

6 I heard the song of triumph
　They sang upon that shore,
　Saying, Jesus has redeemed us
　To suffer nevermore:
　Then, casting his eyes backward
　On the race which he had run,
　He shouted loud, Hosanna,
　Deliverance has come!

THE TEMPERANCE BANNER.—*Webb, Key B flat.*

1 Unfurl the temp'rance banner,
   And fling it to the breeze,
And let the glad hosanna
   Sweep over land and seas:
To God be all the glory
   For what we now behold,—
Oh, let the cheering story
   In ev'ry ear be told.

2 Come, join the noble army,
   Enlist now for the fight;
Maintain our nation's honor,
   Firm stand ye for the right;
Promote the cause of temp'rance,
   T' assist poor, fallen man;
Put on the glorious armor,
   Be foremost in the van.

3 Then rally round the standard,
   And let the work go on,
Until the last dim vestage
   Of intemperance is gone.
Be earnest in the battle,
   Your weapons boldly wield;
You'll surely gain the vict'ry,
   And make the monster yield.

1   SICILY.—E.

1 Guide me, O thou great Jehovah,
   Pilgrim thro' this barren land;
 I am weak, but thou art mighty,
   Hold me with thy powerful hand;
     Bread of heaven,
   Feed me till I want no more.

2 Open now the crystal fountain,
   Whence the healing waters flow;
 Let the fiery, cloudy pillar
   Lead me all my journey through;
     Strong Deliverer,
   Be thou still my strength and shield.

3 When I tread the verge of Jordan,
   Bid my anxious fears subside;
 Bear me thro' the swelling current,
   Land me safe on Canaan's side;
     Songs of praises
   I will ever give to thee.

2   —o—   KEY D.

1 Sweet hour of prayer! sweet hour of prayer!
 That calls me from a world of care,
 And bids me at my Father's throne
 Make all my wants and wishes known:
 In seasons of distress and grief
 My soul has often found relief,
:||: And oft' escaped the tempter's snare
 By thy return, sweet hour of prayer. :||:

2 Sweet hour of prayer! sweet hour of prayer!
 Thy wings shall my petition bear
 To him whose truth and faithfulness
 Engage the waiting soul to bless:
 And since he bids me seek his face,
 Believe his word, and trust his grace,
:||: I'll cast on him my every care,
 And wait for thee, sweet hour of prayer.|:

3   FOUNTAIN.—C.

1 There is a fountain filled with blood
   Drawn from Immanuel's veins,
 And sinners plunged beneath that flood
   Lose all their guilty stains,

2 The dying thief rejoiced to see
   That fountain in his day;
 And there may I, though vile as he,
   Wash all my sins away.

3 E'er since by faith I saw the stream
   Thy flowing wounds supply,
 Redeeming love has been my theme,
   And shall be till I die.

4 Then in a nobler, sweeter song
   I'll sing thy power to save, [tongue
 When this poor, lisping, stammering
   Lies silent in the grave.

4   KEY F.

1 What a Friend we have in Jesus,
   All our sins and griefs to bear!
 What a privilege to carry
   Everything to God in prayer.
 Oh, what peace we often forfeit,
   Oh, what needless pain we bear,
 All because we do not carry
   Everything to God in prayer.

2 Have we trials and temptations?
   Is there trouble anywhere?
 We should never be discouraged,
   Take it to the Lord in prayer.
 Can we find a Friend so faithful,
   Who will all our sorrows share?
 Jesus knows our every weakness,
   Take it to the Lord in prayer.

3 Are we weak and heavy laden,
   Cumbered with a load of care?
 Precious Saviour, still our Refuge,—
   Take it to the Lord in prayer.
 Do thy friends despise, forsake thee?
   Take it to the Lord in prayer;
 In his arms he'll take and shield thee,
   Thou wilt find a solace there.

5   —o—   KEY C.

1 There is a gate that stands ajar,
   And through its portals gleaming,
 A radiance from the cross, afar
   The Saviour's love revealing.

CHO.—*Oh, depth of mercy, can it be,*
   That gate was left ajar for me!
     For me, for me,
   Was left ajar for me!

2 That gate ajar stands free for all
   Who seek through it salvation,—
 The rich and poor, the great and small
   Of every tribe and nation.

3 Press onward, then, tho' foes may frown,
   While mercy's gate is open;
 Accept the cross, and win the crown,
   Love's everlasting token.

6   WOODWORTH.—E♭.

1 Just as I am, without one plea,
 But that thy blood was shed for me,
 And that thou bidd'st me come to thee,
   O Lamb of God, I come, I come.

2 Just as I am, and waiting not
 To rid my soul of one dark blot, [spot,
 To thee, whose blood can cleanse each
   O Lamb of God, I come, I come.

3 Just as I am; thou wilt receive,
 Wilt welcome, pardon, cleanse, relieve;
 Because thy promise I believe,
   O Lamb of God, I come, I come.

My Hope and my Glory.

FANNY J. CROSBY. CHAS. EDW. PRIOR.

1. I am walking with the Lord, and be-lieving in his word, I am happy as a heart can be; I am sing-ing all the day how he washed my sins away Thro' the precious blood he shed for me. O the cross where my Saviour hath bless'd me My hope and my glo-ry shall be;

2. Now my way is growing bright, and my soul is full of light, My Redeemer's guiding hand I see; If a thousand words were mine, I would gladly all resign For the rapture of his love to me.

3. I was once a burdened soul, but my Saviour made me whole, his redemption all my theme shall be; I will sing it till I die, and proclaim beyond the sky What the grace of God has done for me.

D. S.—I am sing-ing all the day how he washed my sins away Thro' the precious blood he shed for me.

Copyright, 1884, by JOHN J. HOOD.

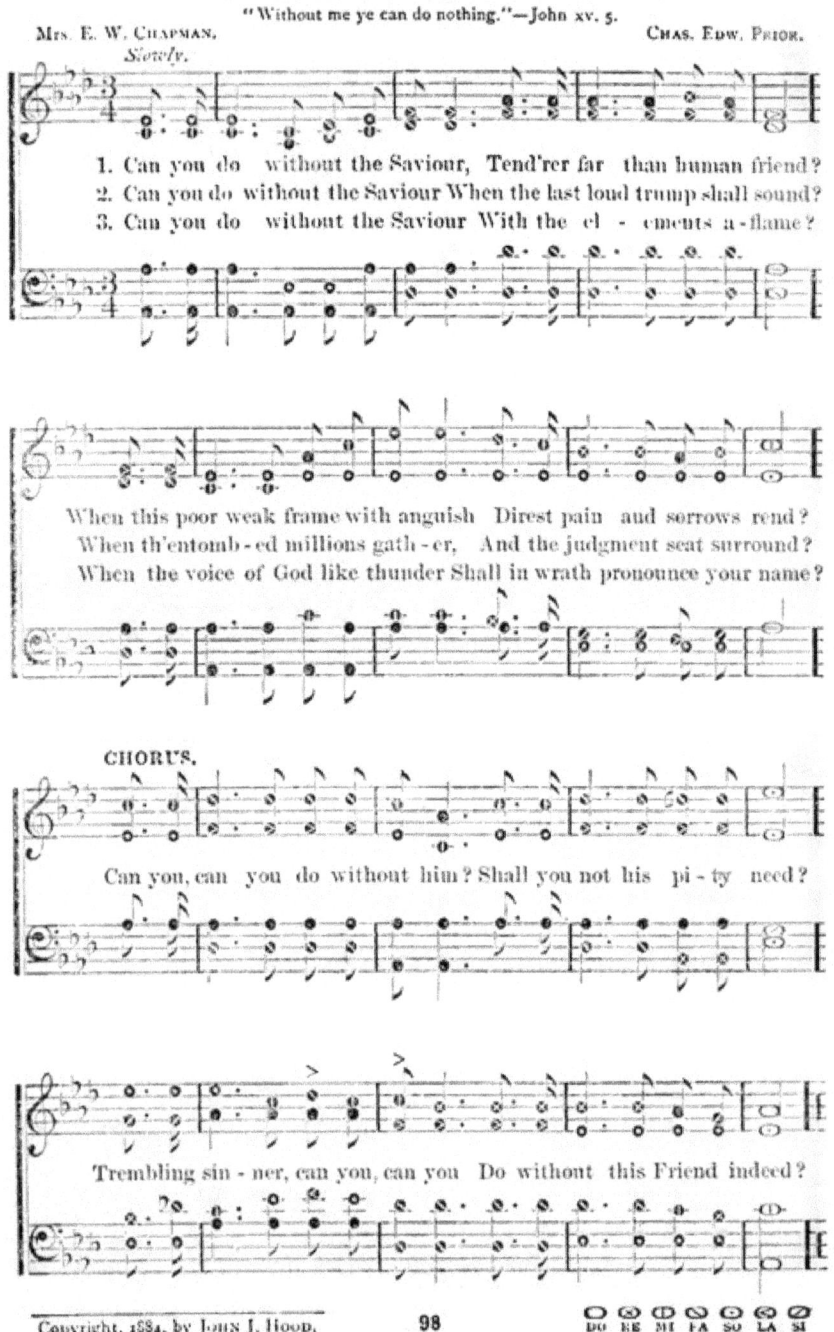

Clinging to the Cross.

Frank Gould. Jno. R. Sweney.

1. O, my heart is full of joy, for my sins are wash'd away, Clinging to the cross of Je-sus; I am trusting more and more in his mercy ev'ry day,
2. I have laid my burden down, I have cast it on the Lord, Clinging to the cross of Je-sus; I can now believe and claim ev'ry promise in his word,
3. I have found the hallow'd peace which the world can never give, Clinging to the cross of Jesus; I have promised by his grace while he spares me I will live
4. I am happy in his love, I am safe beneath his care, Clinging to the cross of Jesus; Tho' temptations I shall meet they shall never harm me there,

CHORUS.

Clinging to the cross of Je-sus. Cling-ing to the cross, where his blood was shed for me, Clinging to the cross, where the flowing stream I see, Clinging to the cross, where I come on bended knee; Blessed, blessed cross of Jesus!

Copyright, 1884, by John J. Hood.

The Countersign.

NOTE.—George H. Stuart, Pres. U. S. Christian Commission, coming from a battlefield, was halted by a picket-guard and ordered to give the countersign. Giving the wrong word he was compelled to return to headquarters. Coming back, and giving the correct word, the guard shouted, "All right, pass on!" Mr. Stuart then asked, "Sentinel, have you *the* countersign?" "Yes." "What is it?" "The blood of Jesus."

Rev. Jno. O. Foster, A. M.   Jno. R. Sweney.

1. In the darkness, as I trod On a wayward, lost de-sign,
2. Trav-'ler, halt! where now you stand There is drawn a dead-ly line;
3. Back to where the words were given, There I sought the love di-vine;

Sud-den-ly a man of God Shout-ed for the coun-ter-sign.
Ere you pass to yon-der land You must give the coun-ter-sign.
When the order came from heaven,"Christ shall be your coun-ter-sign."

CHORUS.

Pass the word from soul to soul, Let it ring a-long the line:

"Je-sus Christ has made me whole!" This shall be my coun-ter-sign.

4 Sentinel, have you the word
  Given from thy God to thee?
Yes, I know the blessed Lord,
  "Th'-blood of Jesus" cleanseth me.

5 Guards will not arrest me now,
  Nothing's wrong within the line;
Heaven's light is on my brow.—
  Christ withing the countersign.

Copyright, 1884, by John J. Hood.

At Home with Jesus.

PRISCILLA J. OWENS.   WM. J. KIRKPATRICK.

1. Our heav'nly habi-tation Above the tempest stands, Where breezes of sal-
va-tion Flow o'er Immanuel's lands; And there, when toil is done, And
peace with vict'ry won, The dawn shall meet life's setting sun, At home, at

2. Tho' here the storms are swelling And floods of sorrow foam, We know we have a
dwell-ing, A sure a-bid-ing home; The Saviour's loving breast Was
pierced to make that rest; O seek this ref-uge, ye distressed, And be at

D. S.—joy and peace for-ev-ermore, At home, at

Fine. CHORUS.   D. S.

home with Je-sus. At home with Je-sus, At home with Jesus, There's

3 His arms of strength shall hold thee
   Above the tempter's snare,
His shadow sweet enfold thee
   Amid the furnace glare.
Pass joyful on thy way,
And in each trial say,
"His presence is my hope and stay,
   At home, at home with Jesus."

4 Across death's rolling river
   True friends have gone before;
We miss them here forever,
   We'll find them on life's shore.
And glad each voice shall blend,
When friend shall welcome friend,
And ceaseless songs of praise ascend,
   At home, at home with Jesus.

Copyright, 1884, by JOHN J. HOOD.

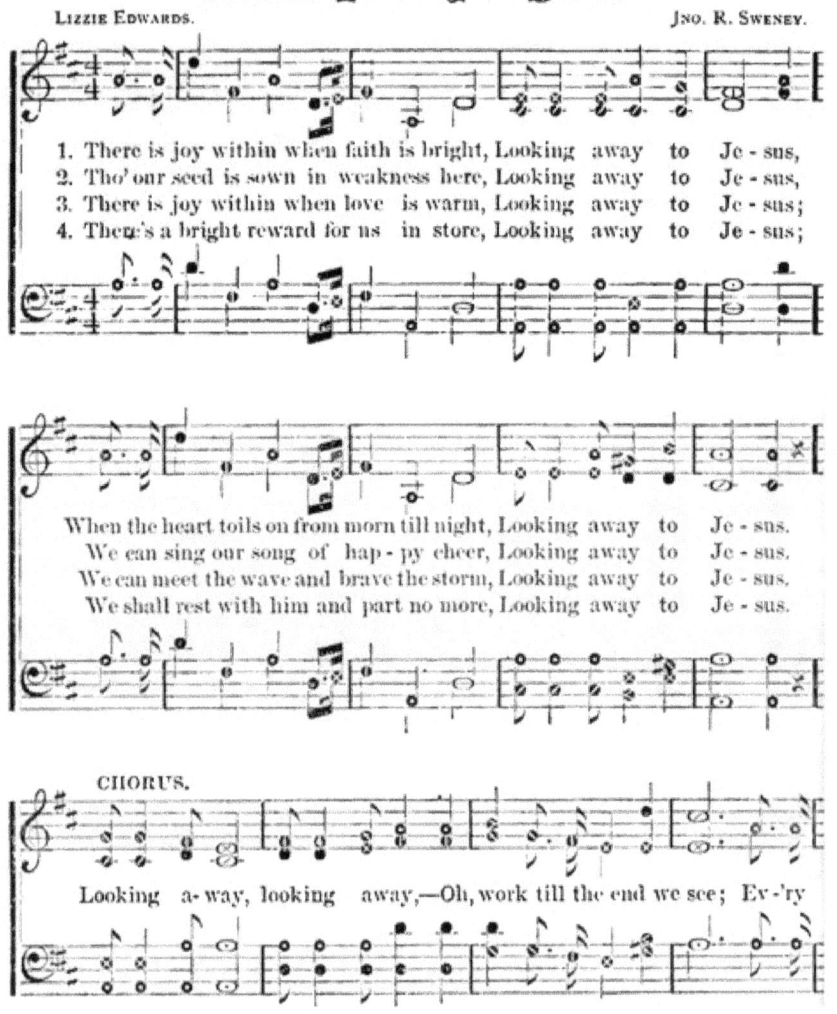

Soldiers of the Cross.

I. Watts. T. C. O'Kane.

1. Am I a sol-dier of the cross,— A foll'wer of the Lamb,— And shall I fear to own his cause, Or blush to speak his name? The conflict's be-
2. Must I be car-ried to the skies On flowery beds of ease; While others fought to win the prize, And sailed thro' bloody seas?
3. Are there no foes for me to face? Must I not stem the flood? Is this vile world a friend to grace, To help me on to God.

CHORUS.

fore us and we must a-rise, To battle for Jesus, his hon-or defend; As-sured of a mansion and crown in the skies, If faithful unto the end.

4 Sure I must fight if I would reign;
  Increase my courage, Lord!
  I'll bear the toil, endure the pain,
  Supported by thy word.

5 Thy saints in all this glorious war
  Shall conquer though they die;
  They see the triumph from afar,—
  By faith they bring it nigh.

Copyright, 1885, by T. C. O'Kane.

DO RE MI FA SO LA SI

Witnessing Spirit. — CONCLUDED.

Light of my heart, Joy of the low-ly, Glo-ry impart!
Light of my heart, of my heart, Joy of the low-ly, the low-ly, Glory, oh, glory impart!

15-197 Flow In.

"He that hath the Son hath life."—1 John v. 12.

Miss Abbie Mills.   Wm. J. Kirkpatrick.

1. O life e-ter-nal, life divine, Help me to grasp the glorious prize;
2. A-bundant life on me bestow, Earth's vapors I would breath no more;
3. Here at thy feet I lay my heart: Make broad the channels for thy grace;
4. O-pen the windows from a-bove And pour thy richest gifts on me;

O life, flow through this heart of mine, From life's pure river in the skies.
Oh, let ce-les-tial breez-es blow, With fragrance laden ev-ermore.
Then fill, and o-ver-flow each part, Enlarge and fill the added space.
More life be-stow, and more of love,—Let me a chosen ves-sel be.

D.S.—My Saviour, life it-self thou art, Thyself possess my waiting heart.

CHORUS.   D. S.

Flow in, flow in, O life di-vine, flow in;
Flow in, flow in, flow in;

Copyright, 1884, by John J. Hood.

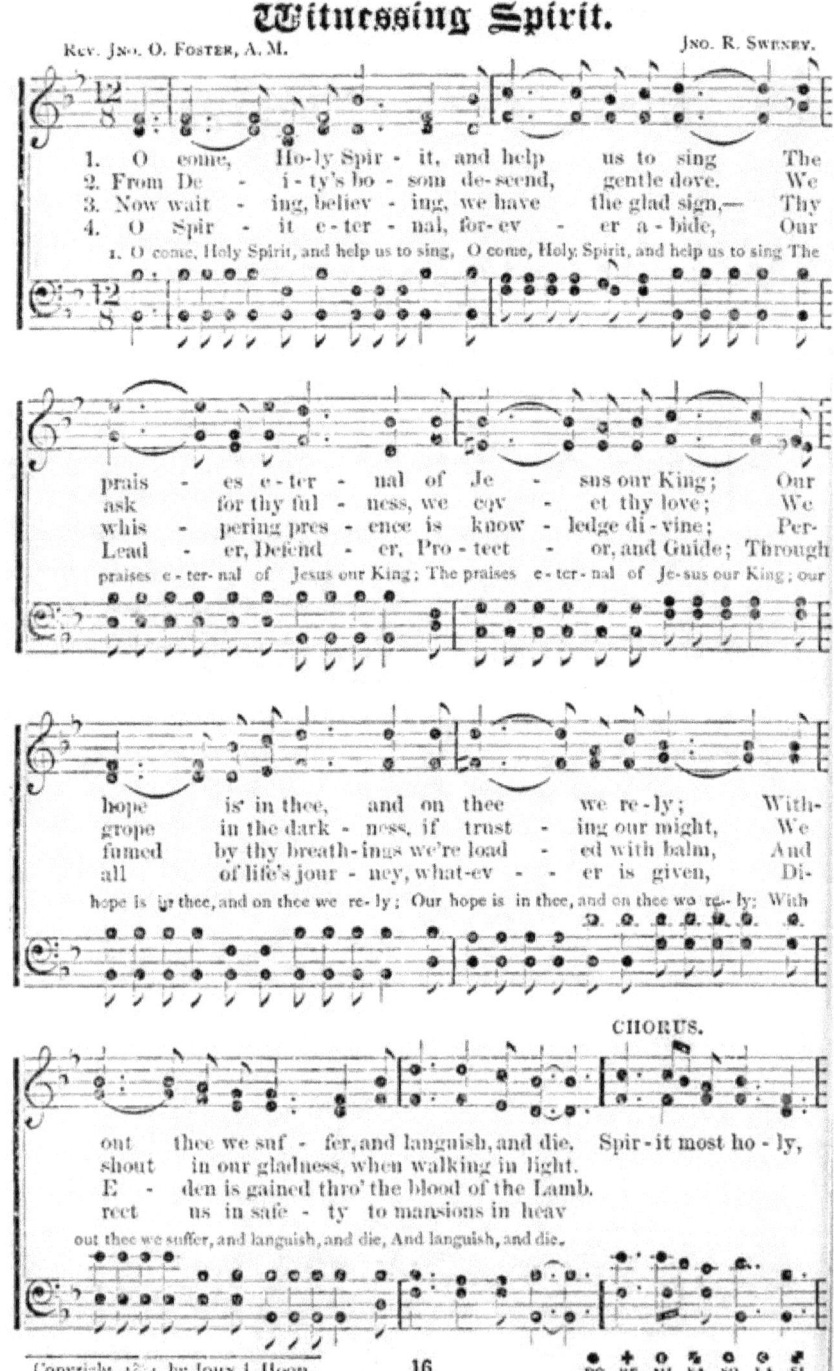

Witnessing Spirit.—CONCLUDED.

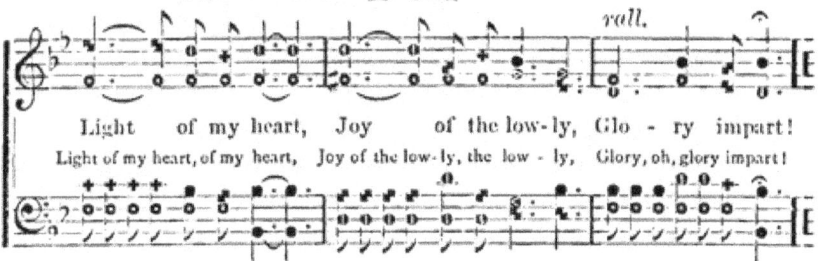

15-197

Flow In.

"He that hath the Son hath life."—1 John v. 12.

Miss Abbie Mills.   Wm. J. Kirkpatrick.

1. O life e-ter-nal, life divine, Help me to grasp the glorious prize;
2. A-bundant life on me bestow, Earth's vapors I would breath no more;
3. Here at thy feet I lay my heart: Make broad the channels for thy grace;
4. O-pen the windows from a-bove And pour thy richest gifts on me;

O life, flow through this heart of mine, From life's pure river in the skies.
Oh, let ce-les-tial breez-es blow, With fragrance laden ev-ermore.
Then fill, and o-ver-flow each part, Enlarge and fill the added space.
More life be-stow, and more of love,—Let me a chosen ves-sel be.

D. S.—My Saviour, life it-self thou art, Thyself possess my waiting heart.

CHORUS.   D. S.

Flow in, flow in, O life di-vine, flow in;
Flow in, flow in,
flow in;

Copyright, 1884, by John J. Hood.

DO RE MI FA SO LA SI

The Fountain Full and Free.

Rev. M. Lowrie Hofford. Thos. Ervin.

1. Ho! ev-'ry one that thirsteth! The fountain full and free,— The fountain of sal-va-tion,—Is flow-ing now for thee. Come, taste the liv-ing wa-ter; Come, take the cup I give: The gift is life e-ter-nal,— Canst thou refuse to live?

2. Ho! ev-'ry one that thirsteth! With ready heart and hand Ac-cept the bless-ing of-fered, Its val-ue un-der-stand. Lift up the voice in ear-nest, And cry, for-ev-er-more: Give me the liv-ing wa-ter, That I may thirst no more.

3. Ho! ev-'ry one that thirsteth! The Spir-it say-eth, Come, The Bride u-nites her gentle voice, And bids thee welcome home. The spring of life e-ter-nal Is opened here for thee, The fountain of sal-va-tion Is flow-ing full and free.

CHORUS.

Ho! ev-'ry one that thirsteth! The fountain full and free,— The fountain of sal-va-tion,—Is flowing now for thee.

Copyright, 1884, by John J. Hood.

Follow Jesus.—CONCLUDED.

Follow Jesus on to Zion: Jesus is a faithful guide.
on to Zion, on to Zion,

50-232 **Lean on Him.**

FANNY J. CROSBY. JNO. R. SWENEY.

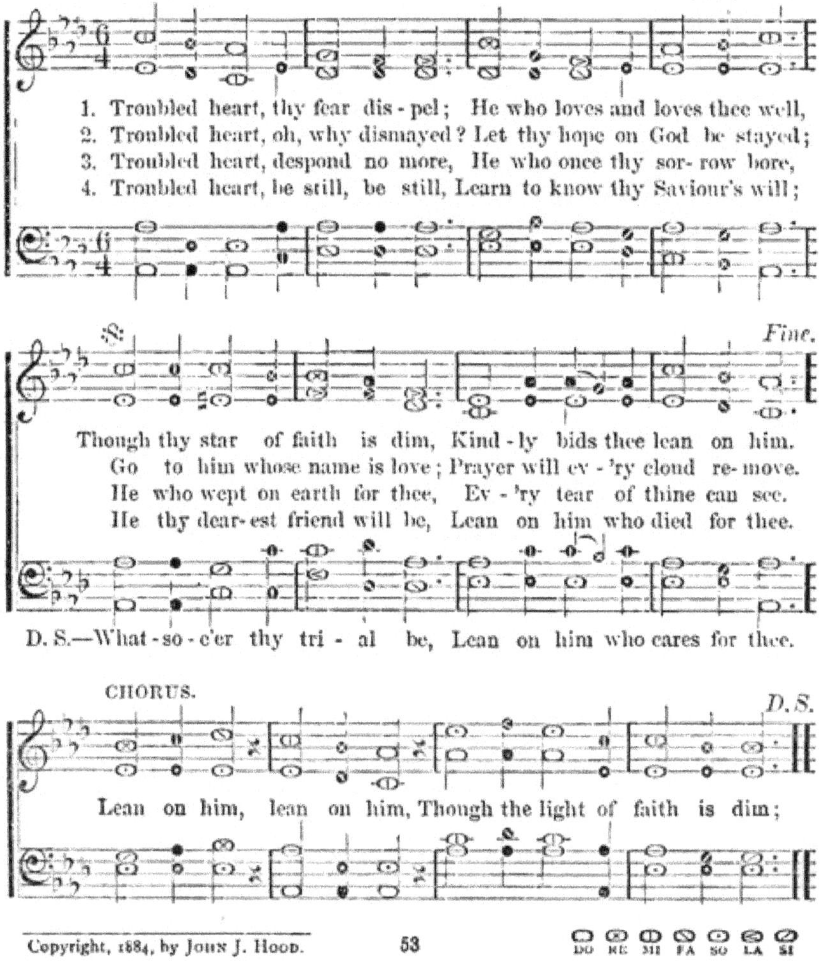

1. Troubled heart, thy fear dispel; He who loves and loves thee well,
2. Troubled heart, oh, why dismayed? Let thy hope on God be stayed;
3. Troubled heart, despond no more, He who once thy sorrow bore,
4. Troubled heart, be still, be still, Learn to know thy Saviour's will;

Though thy star of faith is dim, Kindly bids thee lean on him.
Go to him whose name is love; Prayer will ev-'ry cloud remove.
He who wept on earth for thee, Ev-'ry tear of thine can see.
He thy dearest friend will be, Lean on him who died for thee.

D.S.—What-so-e'er thy trial be, Lean on him who cares for thee.

CHORUS.

Lean on him, lean on him, Though the light of faith is dim;

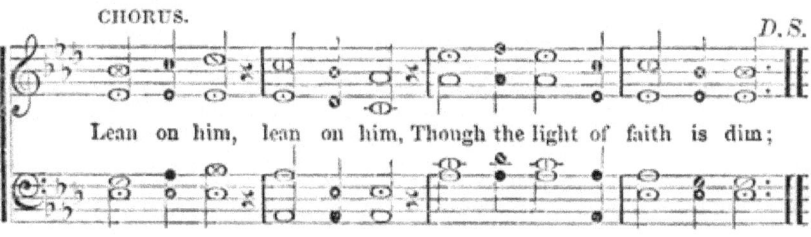

Copyright, 1884, by JOHN J. HOOD.

My Hope and my Glory.

FANNY J. CROSBY. CHAS. EDW. PRIOR.

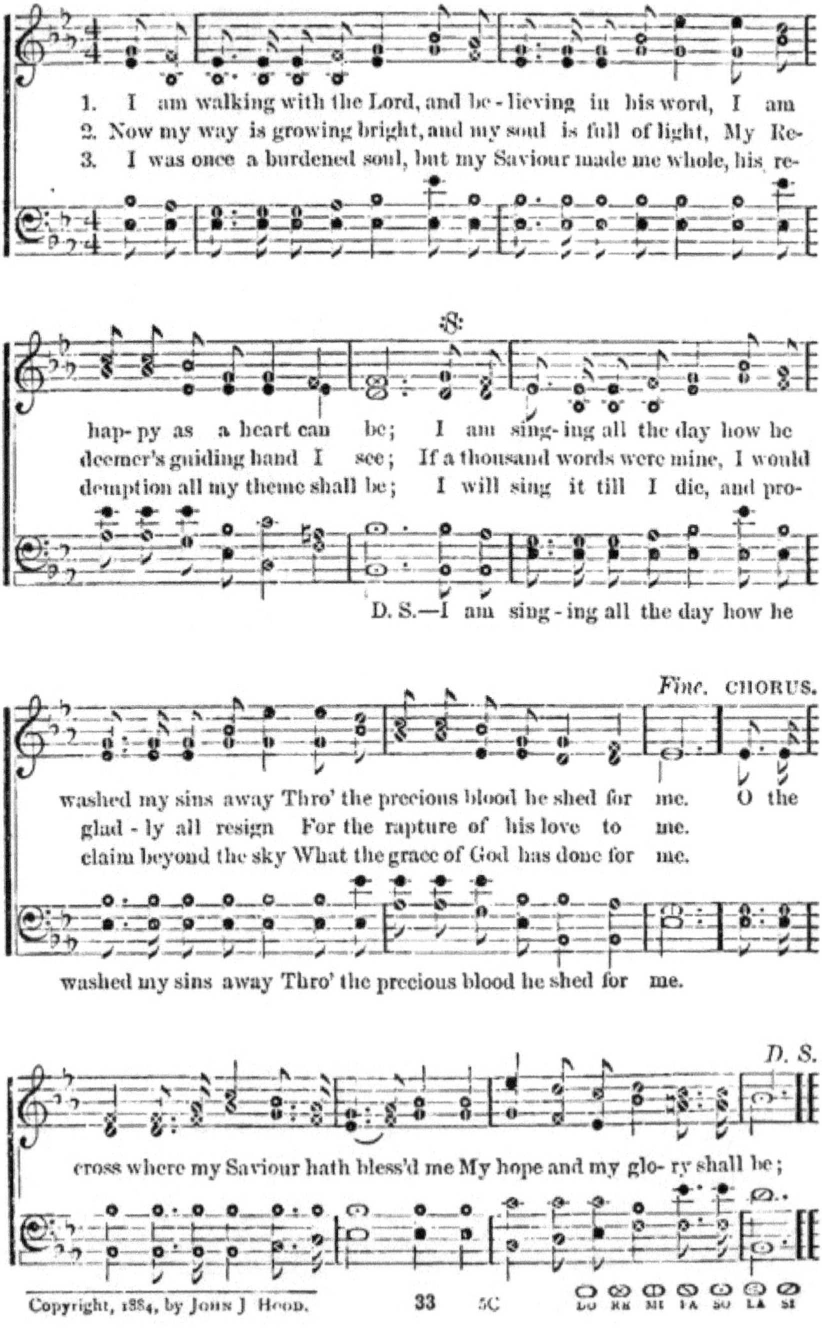

1. I am walking with the Lord, and be-lieving in his word, I am hap-py as a heart can be; I am sing-ing all the day how he washed my sins away Thro' the precious blood he shed for me. O the
2. Now my way is growing bright, and my soul is full of light, My Redeemer's guiding hand I see; If a thousand words were mine, I would glad-ly all resign For the rapture of his love to me.
3. I was once a burdened soul, but my Saviour made me whole, his redemption all my theme shall be; I will sing it till I die, and proclaim beyond the sky What the grace of God has done for me.

D. S.—I am sing-ing all the day how he washed my sins away Thro' the precious blood he shed for me.

Fine. CHORUS.

cross where my Saviour hath bless'd me My hope and my glo-ry shall be;

Copyright, 1884, by JOHN J. HOOD.

Calling for Thee.—CONCLUDED.

Rise, and, like Bethany's daughter, Haste! he is calling for thee.
is calling for thee.

72-254

Jesus our Redeemer.

Frank Gould.   Jno. R. Sweney.

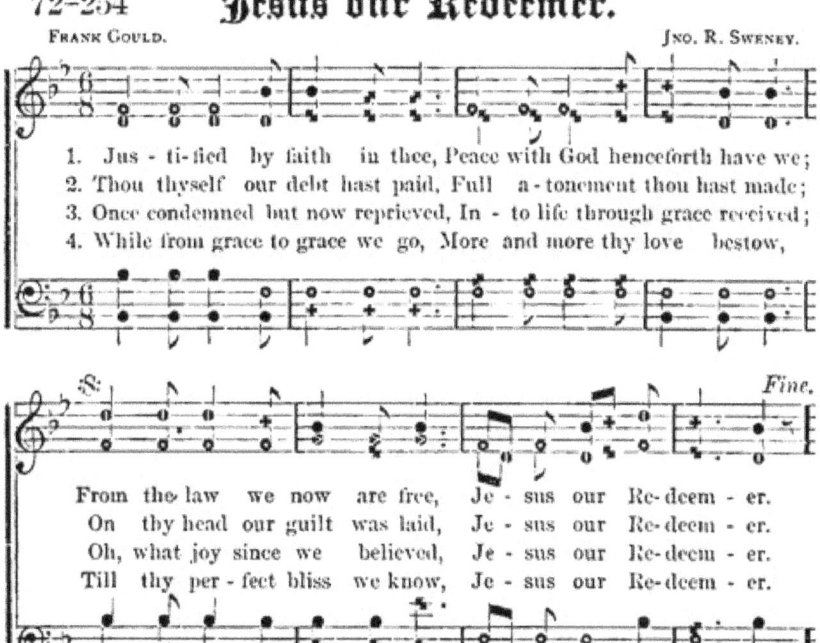

1. Jus-ti-fied by faith in thee, Peace with God henceforth have we;
2. Thou thyself our debt hast paid, Full a-tonement thou hast made;
3. Once condemned but now reprieved, In-to life through grace received;
4. While from grace to grace we go, More and more thy love bestow,

From the law we now are free, Jesus our Redeemer.
On thy head our guilt was laid, Jesus our Redeemer.
Oh, what joy since we believed, Jesus our Redeemer.
Till thy perfect bliss we know, Jesus our Redeemer.

D.S.—From the law we now are free, Jesus our Redeemer.

CHORUS.   D.S.

Not unto us, not unto us, Only thine the praise shall be.

Copyright, 1884, by John J. Hood.

On to the Work.

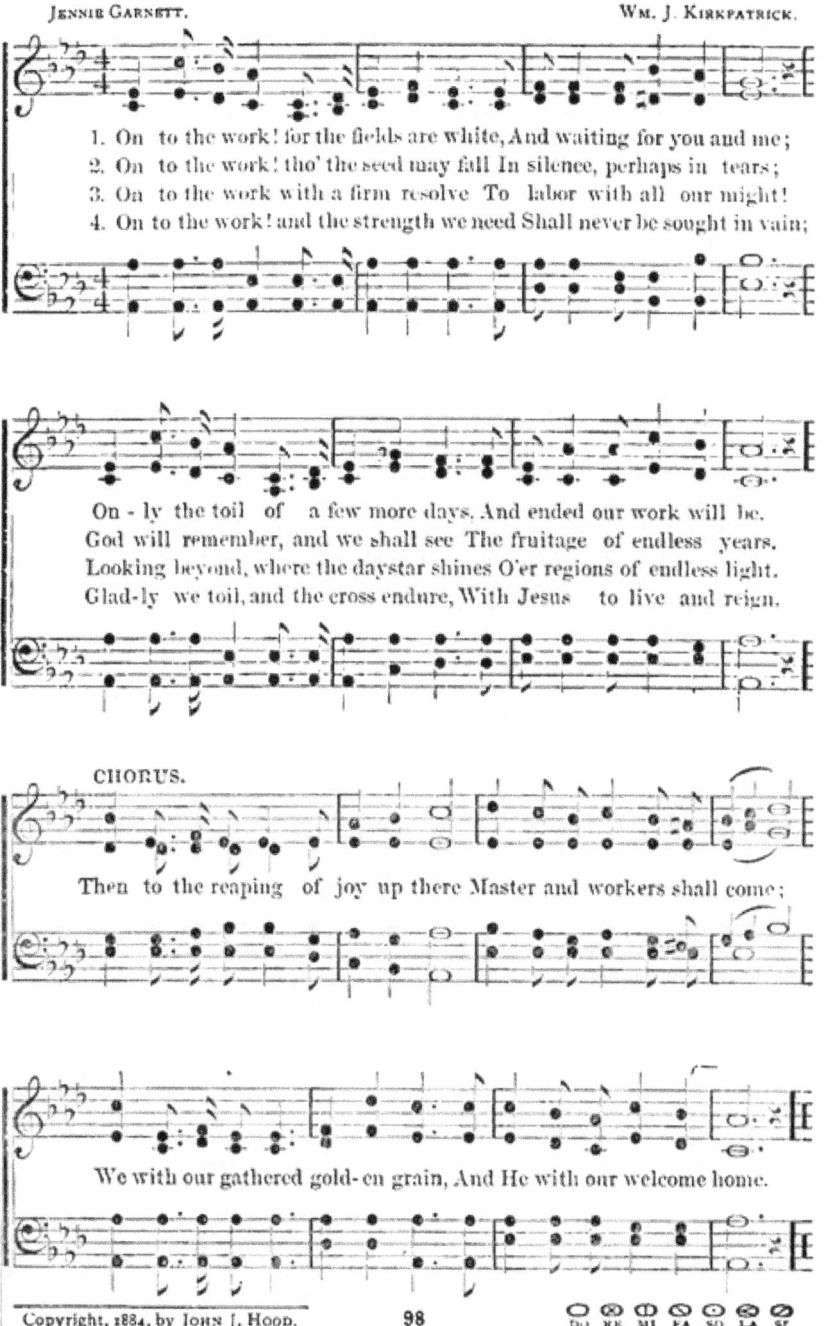

1. On to the work! for the fields are white, And waiting for you and me;
2. On to the work! tho' the seed may fall In silence, perhaps in tears;
3. On to the work with a firm resolve To labor with all our might!
4. On to the work! and the strength we need Shall never be sought in vain;

On-ly the toil of a few more days, And ended our work will be.
God will remember, and we shall see The fruitage of endless years.
Looking beyond, where the daystar shines O'er regions of endless light.
Glad-ly we toil, and the cross endure, With Jesus to live and reign.

CHORUS.
Then to the reaping of joy up there Master and workers shall come;
We with our gathered gold-en grain, And He with our welcome home.

Copyright, 1884, by John J. Hood.

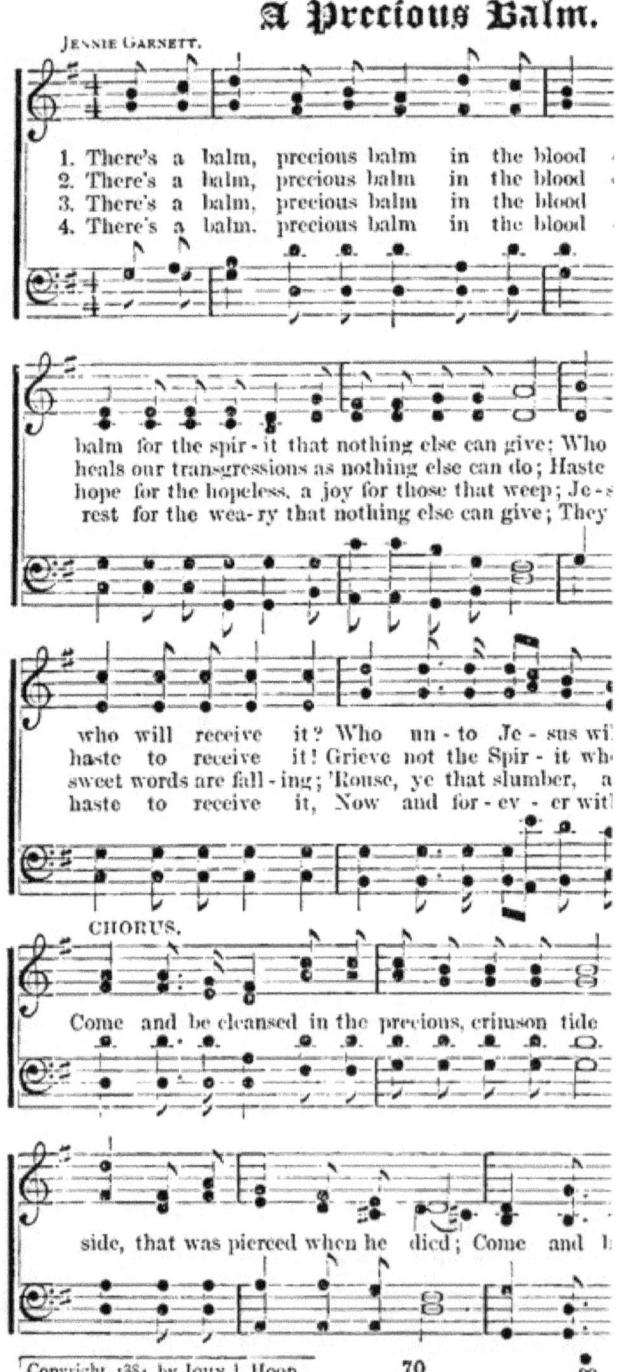

A Precious Balm.—CONCLUDED.

precious, crimson tide Flowing, free-ly flowing from the Saviour's side.

68-250 Holy and Infinite.

FRANCES RIDLEY HAVERGAL. WM. J. KIRKPATRICK.

1. Ho-ly and In-fi-nite! viewless, e-ter-nal! Veiled in the
2. Ho-ly and In-fi-nite! lim-it-less, boundless, All thy per-
3. King of e-ter-ni-ty! what rev-e-la-tion Could the cre-

glo-ry that none can sus-tain, None com-prehend-eth this
fec-tions, and pow-er, and praise; O-cean of mys-ter-y,
at-ed and fi-nite sus-tain, But for thy mar-vel-ous

be-ing su-per-nal, Nor can the heav-en of heav-ens con-tain.
aw-ful and soundless, All thine unsearch-a-ble judgments and ways.
man-i-fes-ta-tion, Godhead in-car-nate in weakness and pain.

4 Therefore archangels and angels a-
   dore thee,
  Cherubim wonder, and seraphs admire;
  Therefore we praise thee, rejoicing be-
   fore thee,
  Joining in rapture the heavenly choir.

5 Glorious in holiness, fearful in
   praises,
  Who shall not fear thee and who shall
   not laud;
  Anthems of glory thy universe raises,
  Holy and Infinite! Father and God.

Copyright, 1854, by JOHN J. HOOD.

THE LATEST POPULAR MUSIC BOOKS.

For the Church Choir.

ANTHEMS AND VOLUNTARIES:

By SWENEY & KIRKPATRICK.

Far in advance of any book of its class for amateur choirs. Becoming very popular.

Price, $1.00 per copy; $10.00 per doz.

THE QUARTET

Embraces all the hymns and music found in the following popular works:—

SONGS OF REDEEMING LOVE,
HYMNS OF THE HEART,
THE ARK OF PRAISE,
QUIVER OF SACRED SONG.

Price, 75 cents per copy; $9.00 per doz. In cloth, gilt, $1.10 per copy, by mail. Words only, $20.00 per 100.

RE-UNION CAROLS:

PATRIOTIC SONGS FOR

DECORATION DAY AND
G. A. R. RE-UNIONS.

Price, 10 cents per copy; $1.00 per doz.

SPICY BREEZES,

By C. W. RAY, D. D., and C. E. PRIOR,

A book of gems of music for the Sabbath-school, has also fifteen Concert Exercises. See this before selecting another book.

Price, 35 cents per copy; $3.60 per doz.

JUST READY!

OUR SABBATH HOME

PRAISE BOOK,

By SWENEY & KIRKPATRICK,

A new and very choice collection of songs for the Sabbath-school.

Price, 35 cents per copy; $3.60 per doz.

THE PLEASANT HOUR,

FOR USE IN

DAY SCHOOLS, SINGING CLASSES, AND THE HOME CIRCLE.

Price, 50 cents per copy; $4.80 per doz.

Harmony Simplified.

TRUE to its title, this work opens up a path to the acquisition of musical knowledge never before dreamed of.

In England HARMONY SIMPLIFIED has made "musicians" of the common people.

HARMONY SIMPLIFIED may be studied in classes or by individuals; the Exercises and Illustrations embrace compositions of the highest order, and are well adapted for use in Music Societies, Conventions, etc.

Price, in cloth, boards, 75 cents.

THE ROYAL FOUNTAIN

IS FOR USE IN

GOSPEL TEMPERANCE,
AND PRAYER MEETINGS.

Price, 10 cents per copy; $1.00 per doz.

Sample copies of above mailed on receipt of retail price.

Philadelphia: JOHN J. HOOD, 1018 Arch St.

PRICE-LIST—MUSIC BOOKS, ETC.

JOHN J. HOOD,

Electrotyper and Publisher of Sacred Music Books,

1018 Arch St., Philadelphia, Pa.

	RETAIL.	PER DOZ.
ANTHEMS AND VOLUNTARIES,	$1.00	$10.00
GOODLY PEARLS, boards,	.35	3.60
THE GARNER, boards,	.35	3.60
" cloth,	.50	
" HYMN EDITION,	.12	1.20
THE QUIVER, boards,	.35	3.60
" cloth,	.50	
" HYMN EDITION,	.12	1.20
GARNER and QUIVER, Combined, boards,	.65	6.60
" " " cloth,	.75	
" " " HYMN EDITION,	.15	1.80
THE ARK OF PRAISE, boards,	.35	3.60
" HYMN EDITION,	.12	1.20
THE TRIO, {GARNER, QUIVER, ARK,} boards,	.85	9.00
cloth,	1.10	12.00
HYMN EDITION,	.25	2.40
THE WELLS OF SALVATION, boards,	.35	3.60
" HYMN EDITION,	.12	1.20
PEERLESS PRAISE, boards,	.35	3.60
SPICY BREEZES, boards,	.35	3.60
SABBATH HOME BOOK OF PRAISE, boards,	.35	3.60
SONGS OF THE NEW LIFE, boards,	.35	3.60
SONGS OF REDEEMING LOVE, boards,	.35	3.60
SONGS OF THE NEW LIFE and REDEEMING LOVE, Combined, boards,	.65	6.60
52 HYMNS OF THE HEART, (With Solos,) cloth,	.25	2.40
THE QUARTET, {S. OF REDEEMING LOVE, THE QUIVER, THE ARK OF PRAISE, HYMNS OF THE HEART,} boards,	.85	9.00
cloth,	1.10	12.00
HYMN EDITION,	.25	2.40
THE ROYAL FOUNTAIN, Nos. 1, or 2, or 3,	.10	1.00
RELIGIOUS SONGS OF THE BUELL FAMILY,	.10	1.00
SACRED ECHOES,	.10	1.00
SONGS OF MY REDEEMER,	.10	1.00
SACRED ECHOES and SONGS OF MY REDEEMER, Combined,	.15	1.50
HEART SONGS,	.10	1.00
MULTUM IN PARVO MUSIC LEAVES, boards,	.40	4.20
HARMONY SIMPLIFIED, cloth,	.75	7.50
THE PLEASANT HOUR, boards,	.50	4.80
FLOWER SONGS FOR DECORATION DAY,	.25	2.40
		PER 100.
HOOD'S CAROLS FOR CHRISTMAS,	.05	4.00
RAY'S CONCERT EXERCISES,	.05	3.00

Retail prices include postage or expressage to any part of the United States or Canada. The rates per dozen or hundred do not include postage or expressage.

To insure promptness in filling orders be careful to remit full amount, either by postal note, check, or draft on New York; if credit is desired give reference in Philadelphia.

www.ingramcontent.com/pod-product-compliance
Lightning Source LLC
Chambersburg PA
CBHW032246080426
42735CB00008B/1026